WORKBOOK

THE BASIC OXFORD

Picture Dictionary

JAYME ADELSON-GOLDSTEIN, FIONA ARMSTRONG, AND NORMA SHAPIRO

OXFORD

UNIVERSITY PRESS

OXFORD
UNIVERSITY PRESS

198 Madison Avenue
New York, NY 10016 USA

Great Clarendon Street
Oxford OX2 6DP England

Oxford New York
Auckland Bangkok Buenos Aires Cape Town Chennai
Dar es Salaam Delhi Hong Kong Istanbul Karachi Kolkata
Kuala Lumpur Madrid Melbourne Mexico City Mumbai
Nairobi São Paulo Shanghai Taipei Tokyo Toronto

OXFORD is a trademark of Oxford University Press.

ISBN 0-19-434567-X

Copyright © 1994 Oxford University Press

Editorial Manager: Susan Lanzano
Developmental Editor: Helen Munch
Editor: Paul Phillips
Designer: John Daly
Production Manager: Abram Hall
Production by Gramercy Book Services, Inc.
Cover Concept by Silver Editions
Cover Illustrations: Craig Attebury, Jim DeLapine, Narda Lebo, Mohammad Mansoor,
Tom Newsom, Bill Thomson
Illustrations: Paulette Bogan, Patrick Girouard, Maj-Britt Hagsted, Karen Loccisano,
M. Chandler Martylewski, Yoshi Miyake, Tom Sperling

Printing (last digit): 20 19 18 17 16 15 14 13

Printed in China

Acknowledgements

Our gratitude is extended to our editor, Helen Munch; our New York support system of Paul Phillips and Martha Torn; and our students, colleagues, and families.

Contents

10. Transportation 76-81

11. Work 82-91

12. Recreation 92-95

Letter to the Teacher

Dear ESOL Teacher,

We hope that you will find *The Basic Oxford Picture Dictionary Workbook* useful with your beginning ESL and EFL students. We have planned it so that the pages can be used in the following ways:

• As homework

For students to do at home, alone or with their families. Answers to the activities are listed in the Answer Key at the back of the book.

• As additional classwork

For those students who finish a class activity early.

• As alternative work

For literacy- or beginning-level students working in small groups with or without a peer tutor.

This student workbook provides follow-up written activities that recycle, in similar and different contexts, the words introduced in *The Basic Oxford Picture Dictionary.* After students use and reuse the words in a variety of ways, they are asked to communicate about themselves, their likes and dislikes, interests, and lives. This information can then be reviewed and discussed in class.

Additional teaching suggestions can be found in *The Basic Oxford Picture Dictionary Teacher's Book.* For communicative listening and speaking activities, as well as additional life skills and narrative reading activities, you may be interested in *The Teacher's Resource Book of Reproducible Activities.* This book features focused listening activities (with an accompanying cassette or CD), information exchanges, interviews, mixers, games and language experience pictures.

All of the related activities and materials will help your students recycle *The Basic Oxford Picture Dictionary* words until they become part of each beginning student's active vocabulary.

We hope you enjoy using this book with your students.

Sincerely,

The Authors

Letter to the Student

Dear Student of English,

We know that you want to remember and use the words in **The Basic Oxford Picture Dictionary**. With this Workbook you will get a lot of practice finding and using the Dictionary words.

Each Dictionary page has a page in the Workbook. The page numbers for both are the same. There are many different activities on each workbook page. There are directions for each activity. The directions look like this:

A. **Look in your dictionary.**

At the end of the Workbook is an Answer Key. Look at the Answer Key when you want to check your work.

At the bottom of some Workbook pages there are questions just for you. Circle or write your own answers when you see this symbol: ★

Show your answers to your friends, family, or teacher. The answers are about you.

Talk to people in English. Use the new words you learn. We know that you can learn English. Good luck!

Sincerely,

Jayme Adelson-Goldstein
Fiona Armstrong
Norma Shapiro
(The Authors)

WORKBOOK

THE BASIC OXFORD

Picture Dictionary

A. **Look in your dictionary.**

How many students do you see? _____

B. **Look at the picture below.**

Write the words on the lines.

> board   book   chair   computer   desk   notebook   student   teacher

a. <u>board</u>

b. _____

c. _____

d. _____

e. _____

f. _____

g. _____

h. _____

C. Write the words in the correct box.

chair   close   computer   desk   listen   look   notebook   open

paper   pen   pencil   point to   sit   stand   talk   window   work

1. Actions	2. Things
close	chair

D. Circle the correct word.

1. I write on   paper   teacher.

2. I read a   student   book.

3. I sit on a   pencil   chair.

4. I look at the   chair   board.

★E. Write about yourself.

I have a _____ and a _____ on my desk.

A. Look in your dictionary.

Match the season to the month.

1. spring	a. January
2. summer	b. October
3. winter	c. May
4. fall	d. August

B. Write in the missing months.

Joe
5/2/68

Mary
4/1/73

Diana
7/3/33

1. Joe's birthday is on _____ May _____ 2nd.
2. Mary's birthday is on _____ 1st.
3. Diana's birthday is on _____ 3rd.

Alex
6/1/01

Rita
10/2/97

Steve
8/3/89

4. Alex's birthday is on _____ 1st.
5. Rita's birthday is on _____ 2nd.
6. Steve's birthday is on _____ 3rd.

★ **C.** Write your answer.

My birthday is on _____ .

5 Time: A Calendar

A. Look in your dictionary.

Write the days of the week on the calendar.

| Friday | Monday | Saturday | Sunday | Tuesday | Thursday | Wednesday |

Sunday						
3	**4**	**5**	**6**	**7**	**8**	**9**

B. Look at the advertisements below.

Circle these words:

day	Friday	Monday	Saturday
today	week	year	yesterday

This week only!
All shoes 25% off.
Come in today!!
Alex's Shoes

Saturday Special!
Lunch only $3.95.

Eli's Burgers

One Day Only!
Once a year sale.
Today's clothes —
Yesterday's prices!
Neil's Clothes for Men

Wanted: ESL Teacher
To Work Monday through Friday.
Nights, 7 – 9 p.m. Good salary.

★**C.** Circle your answer.

When do you go to school?

| Sun. | Mon. | Tue. | Wed. | Thu. | Fri. | Sat. |

A. Look in your dictionary.

Read the clues.

Fill in the puzzle.

```
        4.M           5.M
1.A F T E R N O O N
        │               │
        │               │
      2.E _ _ _   6.N _ _
                    │
                    │
              3.S _ _ _   7.S
                            │
                            │
```

ACROSS

1.

2.

3.

DOWN

4.

5.

6.

7.

★B. Circle your answer.

When do you go to school?

I go to school in the   morning   afternoon   evening.

A. Look in your dictionary.

How many clocks do you see? _____

B. Write the correct time on the clocks below.

> l one   2 two   3 three   4 four   5 five   6 six   7 seven
>
> 8 eight   9 nine   10 ten   l l eleven   12 twelve

l. four o'clock

2. ten o'clock

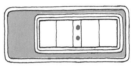

3. two-thirty

4. three-fifteen

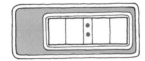

5. seven o'clock

6. eight-fifteen

7. noon

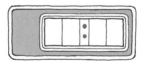

8. nine-thirty

9. one-fifteen

10. five-thirty

l l. midnight

12. eleven o'clock

★C. Write your answer.

What time is it now?

It's _____.

A. Look in your dictionary.

Alphabetize the words that end in **y.**

1. _cloudy_ 2._____ 3._____ 4._____ 5._____

B. Match the clothing pictures to the sentences below.

a.

b.

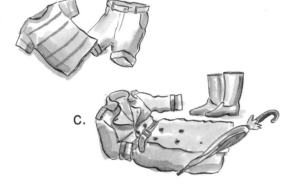

c.

d.

_____ 1. It's raining and cold. _____ 2. It's sunny and hot.

_____ 3. It's windy and cool. _____ 4. It's snowing.

C. Complete the sentences. cold cool freezing hot warm

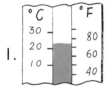 1. It's _warm_ .

2. It's _____ .

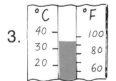 3. It's _____ .

4. It's _____ .

5. It's _____ .

★D. Write your answer.

What's the weather now? It's _____ .

Shapes and Colors

A. Look in your dictionary.

Alphabetize the colors that begin with **b.**

1. _____   2. _____   3. _____   4. _____

B. Write the word in the correct box.

Color	Shape
blue	triangle

C. Look at the classroom on pages 2 and 3 in your dictionary.

Write the colors.

1. The book is _____red_____ . 2. The computer is _____ .

3. The pencil is _____ . 4. The teacher's desk is _____ .

5. The chair is _____ . 6. The board is _____ .

★**D. Circle your answers.**

Is your pencil yellow?	Yes	No
Is your book green?	Yes	No
Is your chair black?	Yes	No

A. Look in your dictionary.

Write the word under the picture.

1. _____

2. _____

3. _____

B. Write the word.

1.

I need 2 _____ .

2.

I need a _____ .

3.

I need a _____

and a _____ .

C. Unscramble the sentences.

1.

Josh's Deli	
adfsd	9.90
bar	4.10
adkrjhf	1.00
Total	$ 15.00

check The for is $15.00

_____ .

Marna Schulberg, M.D.

Date: 3/4/03

Office Visit.............$40.00

for is The $40.00 bill

_____ .

3.

Pearl's Bakery

5¢ 35¢

total $1.75

is The for receipt $1.75

_____ .

★D. Write your answer.

What coins do you have today?

I have _____

A. Look in your dictionary.

Match the word to the picture.

a. 　　b. 　　c. 　　d. 　　e.

1. _____ man
2. _____ woman
3. _____ boy
4. _____ girl
5. _a_ baby

B. Write the words.

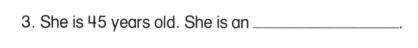

adult　　　　child　　　　teenager

1. She is 10 years old. She is a _____ .

2. He is 17 years old. He's a _____ .

3. She is 45 years old. She is an _____ .

★**C. Write about yourself.**

I am a/an _____ .

I am _____ years old.

A. Look in your dictionary.

Write the number.

How many women do you see? _____ .

B. Write the words in the correct box.

| blond heavy old short tall thin wavy young |

Age	**Hair**	**Height**	**Weight**
old			

C. Look at the picture.

Circle the correct words.

1. My name is Fred. I'm | tall / (short) | and | heavy. / thin. |

2. I'm | young. / middle aged. / old. | I'm 55 years old.

3. My hair is | long / short | and | straight. / curly. |

4. My name is Lucy. I'm | tall / short | and | heavy. / thin. |

5. I'm | young. / middle aged. / old. | I'm 20 years old.

6. My hair is | long / short | and | curly. / short. / wavy. |

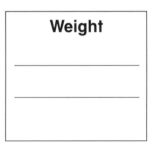

Fred

Lucy

D. **Read the description.**

Draw the hair.

1. short and curly

2. long and straight

3. long and wavy

4. short and straight

5. a long mustache

6. bald with a beard

★E. **Draw yourself.**

Write or circle the correct words.

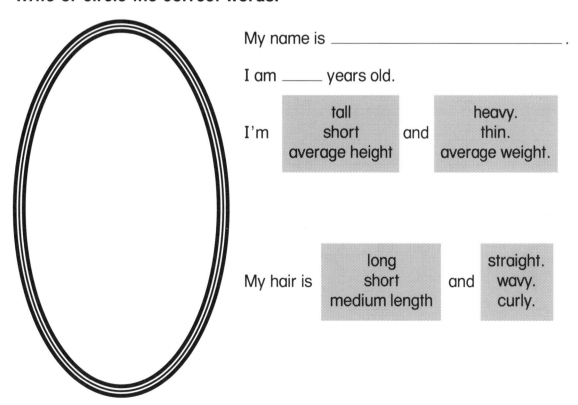

My name is _____ .

I am _____ years old.

I'm
| tall |
| short |
| average height |
and
| heavy. |
| thin. |
| average weight. |

My hair is
| long |
| short |
| medium length |
and
| straight. |
| wavy. |
| curly. |

A. Look in your dictionary.

Alphabetize the words that begin with **c.**

1. _____ 2. _____ 3. _____

B. Write the missing letters.

1.  wa <u>s</u> <u>h</u> your f <u>a</u> ce

2. take a ___ ___ ower

3.  ___ ___ ave

4.  c o ___ ___ your h ___ ___ ___

5. bru ___ ___ your tee ___ ___

6. get dre ___ ___ ed

7. ___ ___ t b ___ e a k f ___ ___ ___

C. Read the story.

Look in your dictionary.

Underline the dictionary words in the story.

My name is Felicia Jones. I <u>wake up</u> at 7:00 a.m.
I take a shower and get dressed. I eat a big breakfast and brush my teeth.
I leave the house at 8:00 a.m. and work from 8:30 a.m. to 4:30 p.m.
I come home at 5:00 and cook dinner. I go to school at 6:30 and
study English. I come home at 9:00 p.m. and go to bed at 10:30 p.m.

D. Write the times from the story.

1. _____7:00_____ 2. _____ 3. _____ to _____

4. _____ 5. _____ 6. _____

★ E. Write about yourself.

I wake up at _____ .   I come home at _____ .

I take a shower at _____ .   I eat dinner at _____ .

I leave the house at _____ .   I go to bed at _____ .

A. Look in your dictionary.

Put the words in the correct box.

Man	Woman	Both
father		
	grandmother	

B. Label the pictures.

brother   daughter   husband   sister   son   wife   mother   father

_____

_____

_____

_____

brother   _____

_____

★**C. Circle the words that are true for you.**

I am

a mother	a sister	an aunt	a niece	a grandparent
a father	a brother	an uncle	a nephew	a cousin

I have

a brother	an uncle	a nephew	a son
a sister	an aunt	a niece	a daughter

A. **Look in your dictionary.**

Answer the questions.

	YES	NO	I DON'T KNOW
1. Is today the boy's birthday?	✓		
2. Is he seven years old?			
3. Is a woman kissing a baby?			
4. Is the boy blowing out candles?			
5. Is the party on Saturday?			

B. **Read the clues.**

Fill in the puzzle.

ACROSS

1. I have two birthday _____ .

5. _____ me the present.

6. _____ out the candles.

7. _____! I want to take your picture.

DOWN

1. Blow out the _____ .

2. Have a birthday _____ .

3. _____ "Happy Birthday to you!"

4. _____ your presents!

A. Look in your dictionary.

Alphabetize the words that end in **y.**

1. _____ 2. _____ 3. _____ 4. _____

B. Write the correct word.

excited	happy	hungry	sad	thirsty	tired

1. She's eating because she's __hungry__ .

2. He's going to sleep because he's _____ .

3. He's laughing because he's _____ .

4. She's crying because she's _____ .

5. He's drinking because he's _____ .

6. She's shouting because she's _____ .

C. Read the story below.

Look in your dictionary.

Underline the dictionary words in the story.

    Mrs. Diego is <u>worried</u> about her family. Her husband is very tired.
He works all the time. Her son, Miguel, is bored. He doesn't like school.
Her daughter, Flora, is homesick. She thinks about Mexico all the time.
The children are embarrassed because their parents don't speak English
all the time. Mr. Diego is sad because his children are not happy.
Mrs. Diego is scared and angry. What is happening to her family?!

D. Write the feelings from the story on the lines below.

Mrs. Diego is . . .	Mr. Diego is . . .	Miguel is . . .	Flora is . . .
worried	_____	_____	_____
_____	_____	_____	_____
_____			

★E. Write about yourself.

How do you feel when you speak English? _____

How do you feel on your birthday? _____

How do you feel now? _____

A. Look in your dictionary.

Answer the questions.

1. Who is graduating, a man or a woman? _____

2. Who is getting a job, a man or a woman? _____

B. Mrs. Sanchez is labeling the photos in her photo album.

Match the photos to the labels.

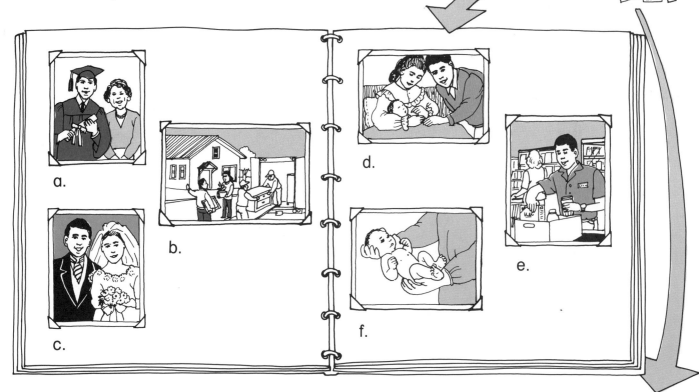

a.

b.

c.

d.

e.

f.

_f_ 1. Julio, born 4/5/69.

___ 2. High School Graduation. (Julio is graduating, Margaret is watching.)

___ 3. Julio's first job at the market.

___ 4. Julio and Margaret. They're getting married!

___ 5. Julio and Margaret's first home. They're moving in!

___ 6. My grandson is born! (Look at the happy parents!)

C. Look at the timeline.

Answer the questions.

1956	1974	1976	1981	1988	1993
born	first job	move to U.S.	married	1st child (girl)	2nd child (boy)

1. When was Margo born?   in 1956

2. When did Margo move to the United States?   _____

3. When did Margo get her first job?   _____

4. When did Margo get married?   _____

5. When was her son born?   _____

6. When was her daughter born?   _____

★ D. Write about yourself.

1. When were you born?   I was born in 19 _____ .

2. When did you move to the U.S.?   I moved to the U.S. in 19 _____ .

3. When did you start school?   I started school in 19 _____ .

4. When did you get your first job? I got my first job in 19 _____ .

5. Are you married?   _____

6. When did you get married?   I got married in 19 _____ .

★ E. Label the timeline with your information.

born

22 Houses and Surroundings

A. **Look in your dictionary.**

Alphabetize the words that begin with **g.**

1. _____ 2. _____ 3. _____

B. **Look at the house.**

Unscramble the sentences.

1. roof the This is

This is the roof _____.

2. the garbage can This is

_____.

3. porch is the This

_____.

4. is the chimney This

_____.

5. is This garage the

_____.

6. driveway is the This , a backyard not

_____.

★**C.** **Circle your answers.**

What kind of house do you want?

I want a house with

a garden	a garage	a patio	a driveway
a porch	a chimney	a deck	a backyard

A. Look in your dictionary.

Fill in the missing letters.

1. The m _a_ _i_ l b o x is in the l ___b b y.

2. A man is talking into the i n t ___ ___ c ___ m.

3. You can take the e l ___ v ___ t o r or the s t ___ ___ r w ___ y to the second floor.

4. If you have a fire, use the f ___ r ___ e s c ___ p ___ to get out.

5. The h ___ l l is outside the apartment doors.

6. When you come into the building, use the ___ n t r ___ n c e.

★ **B. Circle your answers.**

I live in a house.	Yes	No
I live in an apartment.	Yes	No
I have a balcony.	Yes	No
I have a fire escape.	Yes	No
I have a basement.	Yes	No
I have an elevator.	Yes	No

★ **C. Write your answer.**

What's your address?

My address is _____

_____

A. **Look in your dictionary.**

Alphabetize the words that begin with **c.**

1. _____ 2. _____ 3. _____ 4. _____

B. **Look at the picture. Write the words.**

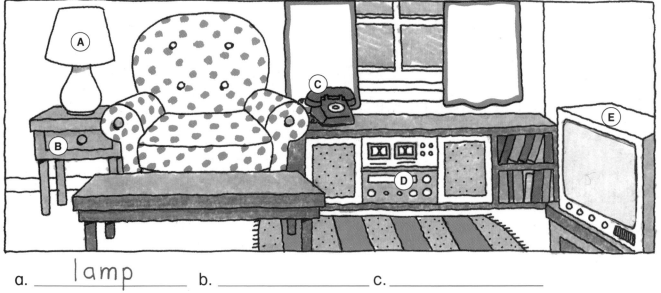

a. _____lamp_____ b. _____ c. _____

d. _____ e. _____

C. **Follow the directions.**

Draw on the living room in B.

Draw a book on the coffee table.

Draw flowers on the drapes.

Draw a cat on the rug.

Draw a picture on the TV.

Draw a newspaper on the floor.

A. Look in your dictionary.

Write the words.

1.

kitchen sink

2.

_____

3.

_____

4.

_____

5.

_____

6.

_____

★B. Write the missing words.

What do you do in your kitchen?

I cook on the _____ and in the _____ .

I put food in the _____ .

I put pots and pans in the _____ .

I wash the dishes in the _____ .

A. Look in your dictionary.

Alphabetize the words that end in **t.**

1. _____ 2. _____ 3. _____ 4. _____

B. Cross out (X) the word that doesn't belong in each line.

1. night table	alarm clock	drawer	bed~~s~~pread
2. blanket	sheets	alarm clock	pillowcase
3. pillow	dresser	closet	drawer
4. curtains	air conditioner	carpet	bedspread

★ C. Follow the directions.

Draw your bedroom. Label the furniture and things in the room.

My Bedroom

A Bathroom

A. Look in your dictionary.

Write the missing words.

hamper   toilet   bathtub   towel   mirror   sink   wastebasket

1. The shower curtain is around the b a t h t u b .

2. The medicine cabinet is over the ___ ___ ___ ___ .

3. The ___ ___ ___ ___ ___ ___ is next to the sink.

4. The man is looking at himself in the ___ ___ ___ ___ ___ ___ .

5. The toilet paper is near the ___ ___ ___ ___ ___ ___ .

6. The ___ ___ ___ ___ ___ ___ ___ ___ ___ ___ ___ is next to the bathtub.

7. The ___ ___ ___ ___ ___ is hanging on the wall.

★B. Circle the words that are true for you.

I take a
| cold | bath | in the morning. |
| hot | shower | at night. |

I have a hamper.	Yes	No
I have a medicine cabinet.	Yes	No
I have a shower curtain.	Yes	No
I have a mirror over the sink.	Yes	No

A. Look in your dictionary.

Write the words in the correct box.

Where do we do this?

make the beds	mow the lawn
plant a tree	rake the leaves
straighten up the room	water the plants
sweep the floor	

In the yard or garden
mow the lawn

In the bedroom

B. Match the picture to the word.

a.

b.

c.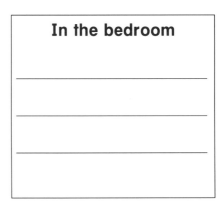

d.

e.

1. __d__ dry the dishes   2. ____ vacuum the rug   3. ____ take out the garbage

4. ____ do the laundry   5. ____ wash the windows

C. **Look in your dictionary. Read the story.**

   Underline the dictionary words in the story.

The Vargas family lives in a big two-story house. Everybody in the family helps clean the house.

On Saturday mornings they are very busy. Olga makes the beds and Pedro cleans the bathroom. The twins straighten up their bedroom.

Mrs. Vargas and her mother wash and dry the breakfast dishes. Carmen dusts the furniture. Mr. Vargas vacuums the rugs downstairs.

Outside, Grandfather waters the plants. He likes to do this on hot days. His grandson Antonio rakes the leaves in the yard. His granddaughter Juana takes out the garbage.

Usually the housework is all done by 10:00, and then everybody can enjoy the weekend.

★D. **Make a check (✓) in the correct box for you.**

	every day	every week	every month	never
I change the sheets				
I clean the bathroom				
I do the laundry				
I wash the dishes				
I mow the lawn				

30 Cleaning Implements

A. Look in your dictionary.

Label the picture.

| broom | brush | bucket | paper towels | rubber gloves | vacuum cleaner |

f. _____

d. _____

b. _____

e. _____

a. broom

c. _____

B. Write the correct word.

1. bucket and ___mop___

2. vacuum cleaner and _____

3. broom and _____

4. sponge and _____

| dustpan |
| cleanser |
| outlet |
| mop |

★**C. Write about yourself.**

What do you use to clean your kitchen floor?

I use a _____ .

What do you use to clean your living room?

I use a _____ .

A. Look in your dictionary.

How many tools do you see? _____

B. Look at the clues.

Fill in the puzzle.

Across

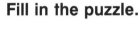

Down

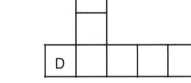

```
        S       H □ □ □
        │       │
  L A W N ■ M O W E R
        │       │     □
        P L □ □ □     □
        │
        □
        │
        □
        │
  D □ □ □
```

★C. Complete the sentences.

1. What tool do you like to use?

   I like to use a _____ .

2. What tool do you want to buy?

   I want to buy a _____ .

A. **Look in your dictionary.**

Match the picture to the word.

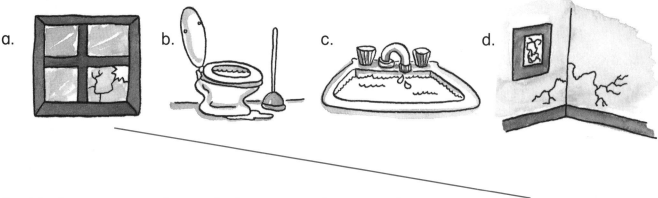

a.   b.   c.   d.

1. dripping   2. cracked   3. stopped up   4. broken

B. **Write the words in the correct box.**

Who do we call about . . .?

| broken steps |
| a dripping faucet |
| a broken window |
| a leaking roof |
| cockroaches |
| a stopped-up toilet |
| a flooded basement |
| mice |

Plumber	**Carpenter**	**Exterminator**
dripping faucet		

C. Look at the picture.

Write the missing words.

1. The _____window_____ is broken.

2. The _____ is stopped up.

3. The _____ are cracked.

4. The _____ is leaking.

5. The _____ is leaking too.

6. The _____ is clogged.

★ D. Write the words and circle your answers.

What problems do you have in your home?

My _____ is   leaking   not working.

My _____ is   cracked   broken.

I have no _____ .

I have   mice   roaches.

A. Look in your dictionary.

Alphabetize the words that begin with c.

1. _____ 2. _____ 3. _____ 4. _____

B. Write the missing words in this recipe.

~~~~~~ *VEGETABLE SOUP* ~~~~~~

1. Fry the _____onions_____ and _____.

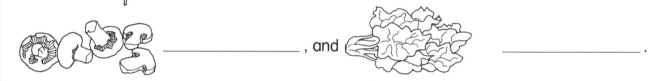

2. Cut up _____, _____,

   _____, and _____.

3. Put all the vegetables into a pot. Add 3 quarts of water and cook slowly.

★**C. Write your answer.**

What vegetables do you put in soup?

_____ _____ _____

_____ _____ _____

A. Look in your dictionary.

Alphabetize the words.

1. _____apples_____   2. _____   3. _____

4. _____   5. _____

B. Write the missing letters in the ads.

1.
Special Sale!

P _E_ AC _H_ _ ES

3 lbs./$1.00

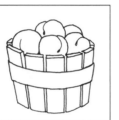

2.
L ___ M O ___ S

5/89¢   this week only!

3.
Don't miss this bargain!

C H ___ R ___ I ___ S

$.79/lb. while supplies last

4.
JUICY, REFRESHING

W A ___ E R ___ E ___ O N!

only 10¢/lb

5.

S T ___ A ___ B E ___ ___ I ___ S

99¢/basket

6.
P ___ ___ M S

39¢/lb.

7.
G R ___ P E ___ R U ___ T

29¢ ea.

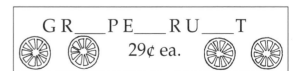

★C. Write your answer.

What fruits do you put in a fruit salad?

_____

A. Look in your dictionary.

How many shrimp do you see? _____

How many clams do you see? _____

B. Cross out (X) the word that doesn't belong in each line.

1.	bacon	la~~m~~b	pork	ham
2.	lobster	shrimp	clams	chicken
3.	beef	fish	steak	ground meat
4.	turkey	lamb	ham	steak

C. Match the food to the restaurant.

A. John's Steak House

B. Hamburger Heaven

C. Marilyn's Clambake

D. Woody's Seafood

E. The Pink Pig Barbeque

F. Millie's Country Fried Chicken

1. ground meat _B_

2. clams _____

3. chicken _____

4. beef _____

5. pork _____

6. fish _____

★D. Write your answer.

What meat do you eat?

_____ _____ _____

What seafood do you eat?

_____ _____ _____

37 Packaging

A. Look in your dictionary.

Draw a line between the words.

Write the words on the line.

1. a|container|of|yogurt   _a container of yogurt_

2. apackageofcookies   _____

3. acartonofmilk   _____

4. abarofsoap   _____

5. abagofflour   _____

B. Write the missing letters in this shopping list.

1. 2 b O X es of cereal
2. 1 j ___ ___ of coffee
3. 2 l ___ ___ ves of bread
4. 3 c ___ ___ s of soup
5. 2 t ___ ___ ___ s of toothpaste
6. 4 r ___ ___ ___ s of toilet paper

★C. **Write your answer.**

In one week . . .

How many loaves of bread do you buy? _____

How many cartons of milk do you buy? _____

How many bottles of soda do you buy? _____

A. Look in your dictionary.

Alphabetize the words that end in **r.**

1. _____ 2. _____ 3. _____ 4. _____

B. Write the words in the correct space below.

> butter   cereal   cheese   cream   ketchup
> mayonnaise   milk   mustard   rice   yogurt

1. Dairy

butter
_____
_____
_____

2. Non-Dairy

_____
_____
_____
_____

> beans   bread   flour   juice   milk
> noodles   oil   soda   soup   spaghetti

3. Liquid

_____
_____
_____
_____

4. Dry

_____
_____
_____
_____

Basic Oxford Picture Dictionary / Workbook

C. Read the doctor's advice.

Circle the food words.

1. You can eat (yogurt) but not (cheese.)
2. You can eat bread but not cookies.
3. You can eat pepper on your eggs but not salt.
4. You can put milk in your cereal but not cream.
5. You can put milk in your coffee but not sugar.
6. You can put margarine on your bread but not butter.

D. Cross out the foods the man can't eat.

> butter   bread   cheese   cookies   margarine
> milk   pepper   salt   cream   sugar   yogurt

★E. Circle your answer.

What do you put in your coffee?

> nothing   milk   sugar   cream   I don't like coffee.

What do you put on your eggs?

> nothing   salt   pepper   I don't like eggs.

A. Look in your dictionary.

How many people are working in the supermarket? _____

B. Unscramble each sentence.

Write the sentence on the line.

1.

customer   a   shopping   is pushing   A   cart

<u>A customer is pushing a shopping</u>
<u>cart</u>

2.

bagger   A   packing   groceries   is

_____

_____

3.

is   The   weighing   checker   the   apples

_____

_____

4.

is   groceries   A   for   customer   paying

_____

_____

C. Read the story below.

Look in your dictionary.

Underline the dictionary words in the story.

Carol and Harry are my best <u>customers</u>. They come here every

Saturday morning. First, they go to the bottle return. Then they take a shopping cart

and push it down the aisles. They pick out the groceries that they need.

They weigh the fruit and vegetables on the scale. They take their groceries

to the checkout counter. I ring up everything on the cash register.

Then Carol and Harry take the bags to their car.

★D. Circle your answers.

Do you go to the market on Saturday?	Yes, I do. No, I don't.
Do you weigh your fruit?	Yes, I do. No, I don't.
Do you carry a shopping basket?	Yes, I do. No, I don't.
Do you push a shopping cart?	Yes, I do. No, I don't.
Do you go to the bottle return?	Yes, I do. No, I don't.

A. Look in your dictionary.

Label the picture.

a. _Saucer_

b. _____

c. _____

d. _____

e. _____

f. _____

g. _____

h. _____

B. Write the missing words.

1. Please give me a _napkin_ .

2. My _____ is missing.

3. I need a _____ .

★**C. Draw and label a table setting at your home.**

43 At a Restaurant

A. Look in your dictionary.

Circle the answers.

1. Is the waitress giving the customers menus? **Yes** No

2. Is the waiter bringing a high chair for a child? Yes No

3. Is the cashier taking money now? Yes No

4. Is the dishwasher carrying the dishes? Yes No

5. Is the cook eating dinner? Yes No

6. Is the busboy smoking. Yes No

B. Write the word in the correct box.

booth busboy cashier chair cook menu waitress water

People who work in a restaurant		Things in a restaurant	
busboy	_____	_____	_____
_____	_____	_____	_____

★ C. Circle your answers.

Do you work in a restaurant? Yes No

Do you eat at restaurants? Yes No

A. Look in your dictionary.

Write the desserts you see.

_____   _____

B. Look at the pictures.

Circle the correct words.

What is he eating for . . .   He's eating . . .

1. breakfast?

scrambled eggs	toast
(fried eggs)	a muffin

2. lunch?

a hamburger	french fries
a sandwich	salad

3. a snack?

 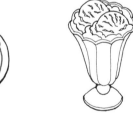

pizza	a donut
a hot dog	ice cream

4. dinner?

spaghetti	mashed potatoes
fried chicken	salad

C. Write the missing letters on the menu.

Norma's Family Restaurant

fr u i t s _ l _ d $1.45   w _ f f l _ s $3.45

fr _ _ d _ g g s $2.55   p _ n c _ k _ s

    with s y r _ p $3.45

s c r _ m b l _ d _ g g s $2.55   with s a u s _ g e

with s _ _ s a g e $3.50   or b _ c o n $4.40

    coffee or tea $ .60

D. Follow the directions.

You are at Norma's Family Restaurant.

You have $5 to buy breakfast.

Write your order and the prices.

Write the total.

Norma's Family Restaurant
Guest Check

Total	

Thank You!

★E. Circle your answers.

What American foods do you like?

I like   hot dogs   hamburgers   pizza   fried chicken

A. Look in your dictionary.

Write five ways to cook food.

<u> fry </u>   _____   _____   _____   _____

B. Read the recipe.

> ### *Fresh Green Salad*
>
> Step 1   Slice the tomatoes and onions.
>
> Step 2   Chop the peppers.
>
> Step 3   Peel the carrots.
>
> Step 4   Grate the carrots.
>
> Step 5   Mix the tomatoes, onions, peppers, carrots, and some lettuce in a big bowl.

Match the steps in the recipe to the pictures.

a.

b.

c.

d.

e.

Step 1 <u> e </u>   Step 2 ____   Step 3 ____   Step 4 ____   Step 5 ____

C. Write the missing words.

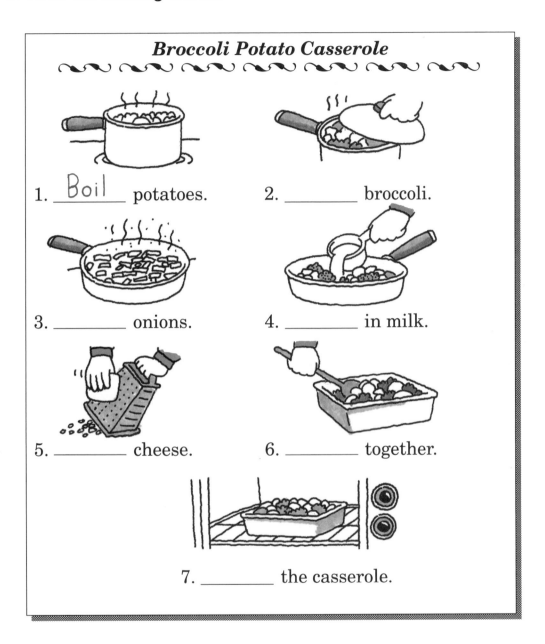

Broccoli Potato Casserole

1. Boil potatoes.

2. _____ broccoli.

3. _____ onions.

4. _____ in milk.

5. _____ cheese.

6. _____ together.

7. _____ the casserole.

★D. Circle your answers.

How do you cook chicken?

I boil bake fry broil it.

How do you cook vegetables?

I boil bake fry steam them.

A. Look in your dictionary.

Circle the answer.

1. Is the police officer wearing a uniform? — (Yes)   No

2. Is everybody wearing shoes? — Yes   No

3. Is a man wearing a cap to work? — Yes   No

4. Is the woman in a dress wearing a belt? — Yes   No

5. Is a man wearing a skirt? — Yes   No

B. Follow the directions.

1. Draw a cap on Mr. Jones.

2. Draw a belt on Mr. Brown.

3. Draw a tie on Mr. Smith.

4. Draw a shirt on Mr. Black.

MR. JONES   MR. SMITH   MR. BROWN   MR. BLACK

★C. Circle your answers.

What are you wearing today?

Today I'm wearing

| pants | a skirt | a dress | a shirt | a belt. |
| shoes | a blouse | a uniform | a suit | a tie. |

49 Casual Clothes

A. Look in your dictionary.

How many swimsuits do you see? _____

B. Alphabetize the names of these casual clothes.

sandals _____

s _____

s _____

s _____

C. Write the missing letters.

1. Let's go for a swim. Put on your s w i m s u i t.

2. The sun is very bright. Put on your s ___ ___ g ___ ___ ___ ___ ___ s.

3. It's too hot for shoes. Put on your s ___ ___ d ___ ___ s.

4. Let's go for a run. Put on your warm-up suit and s ___ ___ ___ k ___ ___ s.

5. Let's go to the park. Put on your T-s ___ ___ ___ t and shorts.

6. The sun is hot. Put on your b ___ ___ ___ b ___ ___ l c ___ p.

★D. Write about yourself.

What do you wear when it's very hot?

I wear _____ and _____.

A. Look in your dictionary.

Alphabetize the words that end in

1. _coat_   2. _____   3. _____

4. _____   5. _____   6. _____

B. Match the word to the picture.

Where do we wear them?

1. earmuffs

a.

2. gloves

b.

3. boots

c.

4. scarf

d.

5. mittens

★**C. Circle your answers.**

What cold weather clothes do you wear here?

I wear
| a jacket | a hat | gloves | a sweatshirt. |
| a coat | a scarf | boots | a raincoat. |

Did you wear cold weather clothes in your country?   Yes   No

A. Look in your dictionary.

Alphabetize the words that begin with p.

1. _____ 2. _____ 3. _____

B. Match the picture to the sentence.

a.   b.   c.   d.   e.   f.   g.   h.

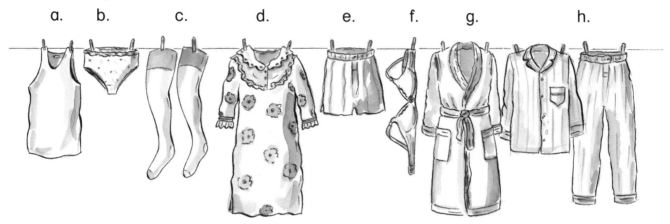

1. This is a bra. _f_

2. This is an undershirt. ____

3. This is a nightgown. ____

4. This is a bathrobe. ____

5. These are boxer shorts. ____

6. These are stockings. ____

7. These are pajamas. ____

8. These are panties. ____

★C. Write your sizes.

I wear size ____ .

I wear size ____ .

I wear size ____

I wear size ____ .

A. Look in your dictionary.

Circle the correct words.

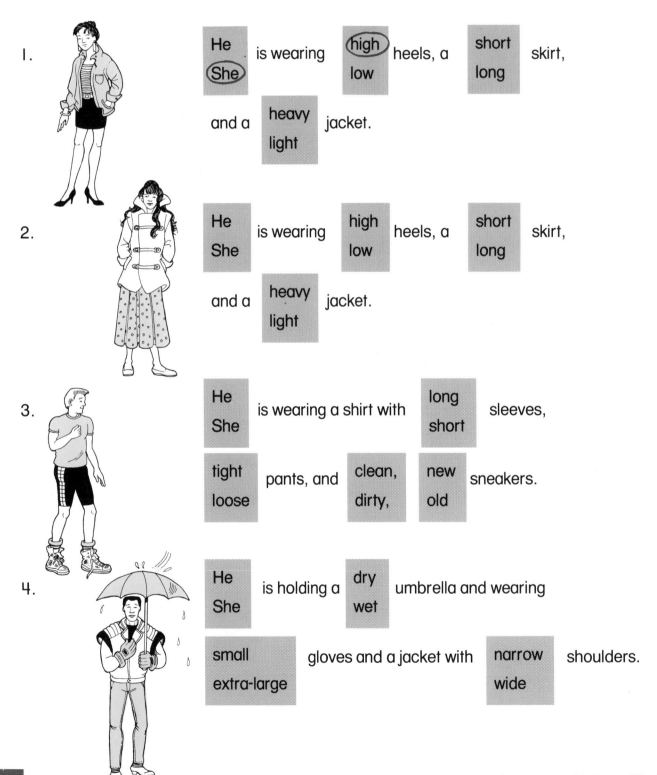

1. He
    (She) is wearing **(high)** / low heels, a short / long skirt,

    and a heavy / light jacket.

2. He
    She is wearing high / low heels, a short / long skirt,

    and a heavy / light jacket.

3. He
    She is wearing a shirt with long / short sleeves,

    tight / loose pants, and clean, / dirty, new / old sneakers.

4. He
    She is holding a dry / wet umbrella and wearing

    small / extra-large gloves and a jacket with narrow / wide shoulders.

B. Look at the clues.

Fill in the puzzle.

1. The opposite of new.

2. The opposite of clean.

3. The opposite of wide.

4. The opposite of light.

5. The opposite of low.

6. The opposite of dry.

7. The opposite of loose.

1. O L D

★ C. Write about yourself.

What size T-shirt do you wear?

small   medium   large   extra-large

What kinds of clothing do you have?

In my closet I have long _____ , short _____ ,

new _____ , and old _____ .

A. Look in your dictionary on pages 49 to 51.

Write the correct words under the picture.

1. ___sneakers___   2. _____   3. _____   4. _____

B. Look at the pictures.

Write the words.

1. 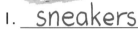 The sandal is ___between_____ the sneakers.

2.  The sandal is _____ _____ _____ the slippers.

3.  The sandal is _____ the boot.

4.  The sandal is _____ the sneaker.

C. Follow the directions.

Draw a shoe on the line.

Write S above the shoe.

Write H next to the shoe.   _____

Write O on the shoe.

Write E below the shoe.

★D. Write about yourself.

What size shoe do you wear? Size _____

Jewelry and Accessories

A. Look in your dictionary.

   Draw the item.

   a watch _____   glasses _____   a wallet _____

B. Label the ad.

~ *Bijoux Jewelry Store* ~

SALE

1. _ring_ _____ $35   2. _____ $15

3. _____ $25

4. _____ $10   5. _____ $40

★**C. Look at the ad.**

   You have $100. Write the items you want to buy. Write the total.

   _____ $ _____

   _____ $ _____

   _____ $ _____

   _____ $ _____

   Total $ _____

A. Look in your dictionary.

How many washing machines do you see? _____

How many dryers do you see? _____

B. Write the order: 1st, 2nd, 3rd, 4th, 5th.

_____ Fold the clothes.

_____ Unload the machine.

___1st_____ Load the machine.

_____ Put detergent in the machine.

_____ Put clothes in the dryer.

★C. Write about yourself.

Who washes your clothes? _____

Where? | at home |
         | at the laundromat |

A. Look in your dictionary.

Write the words.

 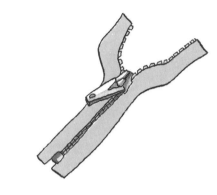 

1. scissors   2. _____   3. _____

4. _____   5. _____   6. _____

★B. Circle your answers.

I like to hang up my clothes.	Yes	No
I like to try on new clothes.	Yes	No
I like to sew clothes.	Yes	No
I like to alter clothes.	Yes	No
I like to lengthen pants.	Yes	No
I like to shorten skirts.	Yes	No

A. Look in your dictionary.

1. What color is the man's shirt? _____

2. Are the dancers heavy or thin? _____

B. Look in your dictionary.

Write the words in the correct box.

fingers	back	legs	arms	feet	chest	neck	head	toes	hips

I have one . . .	I have two . . .	I have ten . . .
		fingers

C. Cross out (X) the word that doesn't belong in each line.

1. foot   toe   heel   ch̶e̶s̶t̶

2. finger   ankle   thumb   hand

3. knee   chest   back   waist

4. arm   wrist   hip   elbow

5. calf   knee   thigh   wrist

D. Write the missing words.

This is what we say in English.

1.

He's very kind.
He has a big

h e a r t .

2.

She's very smart.
She's a real

____ ____ ____ ____ ____ ____ .

3.

That smell doesn't bother him. He has a strong

____ ____ ____ ____ ____ ____ ____ .

4.

Listen to that baby cry.
He has a good set of

____ ____ ____ ____ ____ .

★E. Circle the words that are true for you.

I have
- a strong stomach.
- a big heart.
- a good set of lungs.

A. Look in your dictionary and label the picture.

a. <u>forehead</u>

b. _____

c. _____

d. _____

e. _____

f. _____

g. _____

h. _____

B. Read the letter.

Look in your dictionary.

Underline the dictionary words in the letter.

Dear Aunt Jane,

   Here's a picture of our Tanya. Isn't she beautiful? She has her father's <u>eyes</u> and mouth. She has my nose, not too big, not too small. Maybe she will have the family ears. They are quite big. Can you see her tooth? It's her first tooth. I love it. Her chin is really cute, too.

              With love,
                 Julie

★C. Look in the mirror.

Draw your face.

Label it.

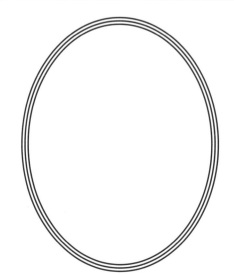

61 Toiletries

A. Look in your dictionary.

Alphabetize the words with **sh.**

1. _brush_   2. _____   3. _____   4. _____   5. _____

B. Write the words under the correct pictures.

blades   brush   comb   toothbrush   razor   toothpaste   shampoo

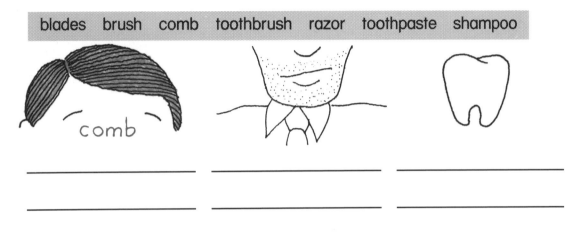

comb

_____   _____   _____

_____   _____   _____

_____

★C. Circle the toiletries you need to buy this week.

Shopping List

shampoo

toothpaste

toothbrush

deodorant

shaving cream

blades

razor

comb

A. Look in your dictionary.

Alphabetize the words that end in ache.

1. backache   2. _____   3. _____   4. _____   5. _____

B. Read the story.

Look in your dictionary.

Underline the dictionary words in the story.

What's the Matter?

Thot Sok is absent from class today. He has a <u>cold</u> and a sore throat.

He is coughing and sneezing. He has a headache and a fever. He is in bed.

His daughter Tu is home too. She has an insect bite on her foot.

Her ankle is swollen and her toe is infected. She cannot walk,

so she's in bed too.

Thot's wife is at the doctor's today. She has high blood pressure

and sometimes she faints.

Who's taking care of the baby? He has a stomachache.

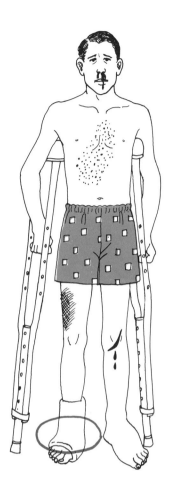

C. Follow the directions.

Mark the picture.

This man has many problems.

He had an accident.

1. Circle his broken ankle.

2. Make an X on his bloody nose.

3. Write the letter R on his rash.

4. <u>Underline</u> his swollen foot.

5. Check (✓) the bruise on his thigh.

6. Draw a Band-Aid on the bloody cut on his knee.

★D. Write about yourself.

How are you?   Fine   So-so   Not so good   Sick

Do you have high blood pressure?   Yes   No

Do you have any aches and pains?   Yes   No

What's the matter? I have $\begin{smallmatrix} a \\ an \end{smallmatrix}$ _____ .

A. Look in your dictionary.

How many kinds of medicine do you see? _____

B. Match the problems to the treatment.

WHEN YOU HAVE . . .	YOU GET . . .

1. 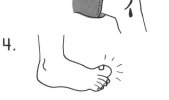 a. cream/ointment

2. b. pills and exercises

3. c. a cast

4. d. an injection

5. e. stitches

★C. Circle your answers.

IN THE PAST

Did you ever have an operation?	Yes	No
Did you ever get a cast?	Yes	No
Did you ever get stitches?	Yes	No

NOW

Do you exercise?	Yes	No
Do you take medicine?	Yes	No

65 First Aid and Health Care Items

A. **Look in your dictionary.**

Fill in the correct word.

1. He has a broken leg.   Give him some ___crutches___ .

2. She has a backache.   Give her a _____ .

3. He has a fever.   Get the _____ .

4. He has a cut.   Get a _____ .

5. He has a bloody nose.   Put on an _____ .

6. She has a stomachache. Give her a _____ .

7. He cannot walk.   Get him a _____ .

★**B.** **Circle your answers.**

What health care items do you have in your home?

Band-Aids	bandage	thermometer	hot water bottle	wheelchair
cotton balls	ice pack	heating pad	crutches	

A. Look in your dictionary.

Circle the answer.

1. Who examines the patient?

2. Who takes a temperature?

3. Who weighs the patient?

4. Who writes a prescription?

(doctor)	nurse
doctor	nurse
doctor	nurse
doctor	nurse

B. Match the picture to the word.

a.
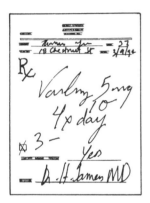

b.

c.
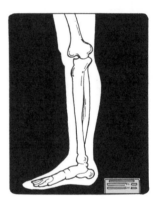

d.

e.

f.

1. patient _b_

4. X ray ____

2. doctor ____

5. insurance card ____

3. receptionist ____

6. prescription ____

C. Write what the receptionist asks a patient to do.

1.  Please <u>show</u> me your insurance <u>card</u> .

2.  Please _____ your _____ .

3.  Please _____ _____ this _____ .

4.  Please _____ your _____ .

5.  Please _____ in the _____ room.

★D. Circle your answer.

Do you have an insurance card?   Yes   No

Do you take prescription medicine?   Yes   No

A. Look in your dictionary.

Fill in the missing letters.

1. p <u>o</u> <u>l</u> <u>i</u> <u>c</u> e station   2. b ___ ___ station

3. f ___ r ___ house   4. t ___ a ___ n station

B. Look at the map.

Write the missing letters.

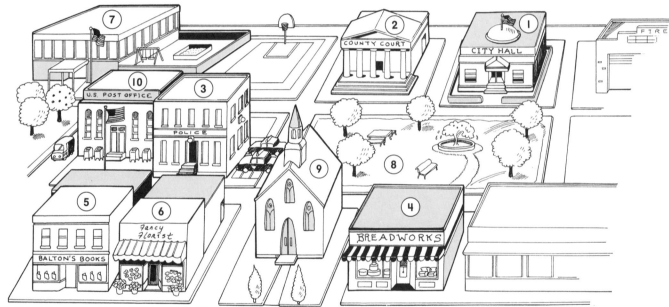

Key

1. c <u>i</u> t <u>y</u> h <u>a</u> ll   6. ___ ___ o r i ___ ___

2. c ___ ___ r t h ___ ___ s ___   7. — — — o o l

3. p ___ l ___ c ___ st ___ t ___ ___ n   8. p a ___ ___ ___

4. b ___ k ___ r ___   9. ___ ___ u r ___ ___ ___

5. b ___ ___ k s t ___ r ___   10. p o ___ ___ o ___ ___ i ___ e

C. Read the story.

Look in your dictionary.

Underline the dictionary words in the story.

On Saturday mornings the King family drives downtown. They park the car in the parking garage across from the post office. The Kings walk to the park and eat their lunch. After lunch they drive to the mall. First they go shopping at Stockton's department store. Then they go to the movie theater. After the movie, they stop at the bakery and buy some donuts. It's late in the afternoon when the tired but happy King family drives back home.

D. Read the story again and number the pictures in the correct order.

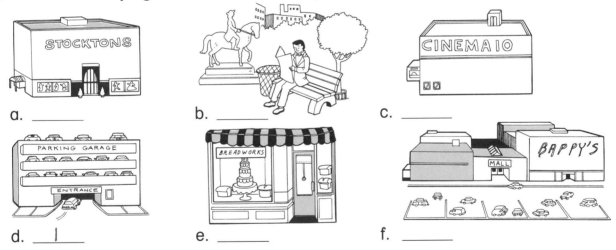

a. _____

b. _____

c. _____

d. __|____

e. _____

f. _____

★E. Circle the words that are true for you.

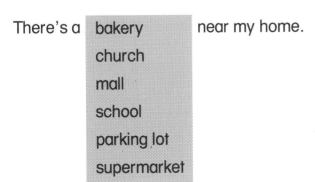

There's a | bakery | near my home.

bakery
church
mall
school
parking lot
supermarket

A. Look in your dictionary.

Write the words in the correct space below.

> amount   ATM/cash machine   date   drive-thru window
> line   security guard   signature   teller

Places you wait at the bank	Jobs at the bank	Things you write on a check
ATM/cash machine	_____	_____
_____	_____	_____
_____		_____

B. Look at the bank book and the questions below.

Write the answers.

Deposits/Withdrawals		Amount	Date
Deposit	$	55.00	7/2/04
Service charge		2.00	7/19/04
Withdrawal		15.00	7/21/04

1. What's the amount of the deposit? _____

2. What's the date of the deposit? _____

3. What's the date of the withdrawal? _____

4. What's the amount of the withdrawal? _____

★C. Circle your answer.

Where do you keep your money?

> in the bank   in my pocket   at home   under the bed

The Post Office

A. Look at your dictionary.

Alphabetize the words that end in e.

1. _____   2. _____   3. _____

B. Complete the sentences.

1. Letter carriers deliver . . .   ____ a. mailbox.

2. Postal workers sell . . .   ____ b. return address on the envelope.

3. Mail your letters in the . . .   ____ c. stamps and money orders.

4. Don't forget to write your . . .   _I_ d. letters, postcards, and packages.

★C. Follow the directions.

1. Write your address and zip code on the postcard.

Miami Beach at Night

Hi!
We're having a
great time. I
hope you're well.
See you soon.

Jennifer

2. Write your return address on the envelope.

Mr. Joe Budd

A. Look in your dictionary.

Write the number.

1. How many people are at the bus stop? _____

2. How many people are in the street? _____

B. Look in your dictionary.

Match the location to the action.

1. bus stop   _____ a. cross

2. crosswalk   _____ b. stop

3. mailbox   __|__ c. wait for the bus

4. public telephone   _____ d. mail a letter

5. sidewalk   _____ e. walk

6. traffic light   _____ f. make a phone call

C. Label the picture.

D. Read the sentence.

Circle the correct picture.

1. He's going into the store.

2. She's looking at the windows.

3. He's waiting for the bus.

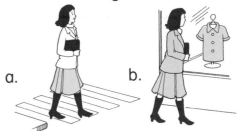

4. She's crossing the street.

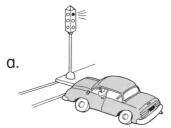 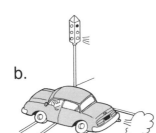

5. The car's stopping.

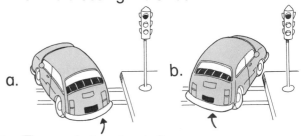

6. The car's turning left.

★E. Answer the questions about an intersection near you.

1. What are the names of the streets at an intersection near you?

_____ and _____ .

2. Is there a traffic light at this intersection?

Yes, there is.   No, there isn't.

3. Is there a bus stop at this intersection?

Yes, there is.   No, there isn't.

4. Is there a crosswalk at this intersection?

Yes, there is.   No, there isn't.

A. Look in your dictionary.

Write the words in the correct box.

| accident | fire | fire fighter | mugging |
| paramedic | police officer | robbery |

Emergencies	**Occupations**
accident	

B. Label the natural disasters.

1. tornado

2. _____

3. _____

4. _____

★C. Circle the words that are true for you.

I know what to do in

a flood.
a hurricane.
a tornado.
a fire.
an earthquake.

D. Look at the picture.

Write the correct words.

1. Be careful! Don't eat so fast.

   You don't want to _choke_ .

2. Watch your step!
   You don't want to _____ .

3. Don't go swimming in that lake!

   You don't want to _____ .

4. Call the paramedics!
   This man is having a

   _____ _____ .

5. Lock the cabinets!
   You don't want the children to

   _____ _____ .

6. Put away those matches!
   We don't want to start a _____ .

A. Look in your dictionary.

Answer the questions.

What color is the van? _____ What color is the truck? _____

B. Look at the picture.

Write the word.   bus   bicycle   car   motorcycle   plane   taxi cab

1. He drives a ___car___ .

2. She rides a _____ .

3. They take the _____ .

4. He rides a _____ .

5. She flies a _____ .

6. He drives a _____ .

★C. Circle your answer.

How did you come to this country?

by car   by bus   by plane   by train   by ship

Basic Oxford Picture Dictionary / Workbook

Parts of a Car

A. Look in your dictionary.

Write the words in the correct box.

On the car	Inside the car
license plate	

accelerator   dashboard   license plate
steering wheel   tire   windshield

B. Read the clues.

Fill in the puzzle.

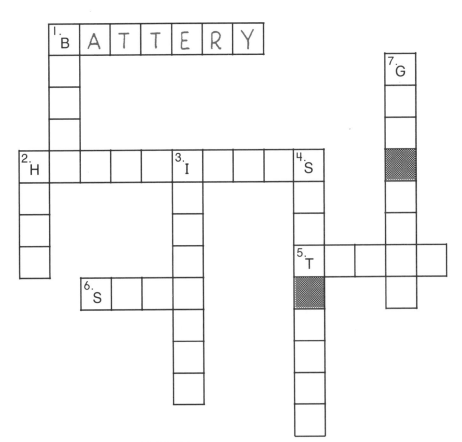

ACROSS

1. The car doesn't start. The ___ is dead.

2. It's dark. Turn on your ___ .

5. Put the groceries in the ___ .

6. Put the baby in the car ___ .

DOWN

1. Red light! Put your foot on the ___ .

2. Look under the ___ .

3. Start the car. First put the key in the ___ .

4. Don't start the car! Put on your ___ .

7. Did you fill the ___ ?

A. Look in your dictionary.

Write the answers.

1. What color is the car going up the hill? _____

2. What color is the car pulling into the gas station? _____

3. What color is the car going down the hill? _____

B. Match the picture to the description.

a.
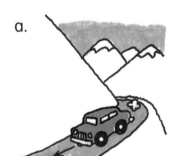

b.

c.

d.

e.

f.

1. around the
   mountain
   ___C___

2. away from
   the hill
   _____

3. down the
   mountain
   _____

4. over the
   hill
   _____

5. toward the
   mountain
   _____

6. up the
   hill
   _____

C. Look at the picture.

Unscramble the sentences.

1. walks the from He away school.

He walks away from the school.

2. across walks the He street.

_____

3. toward He walks the market.

_____

4. into the goes He market.

_____

5. walks the He out market of.

_____

6. the He around corner goes.

_____

7. up walks steps and into He the house the.

_____

D. Circle your answers.

1. When you go to school, do you go over a bridge?

    Yes, I do.   No, I don't.

2. When you go toward your home, do you go up a hill?

    Yes, I do.   No, I don't.

A. Look in your dictionary.

Alphabetize the words that end in **e.**

1. _arrive_ 2. _____ 3. _____ 4. _____

5. _____ 6. _____ 7. _____ 8. _____

B. Write the missing letters in each sign.

1.
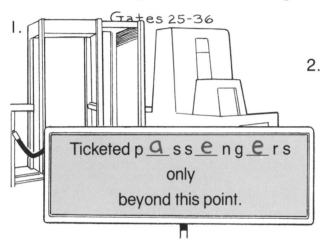
Gates 25-36

Ticketed p a ss e ng e r s
only
beyond this point.

2.
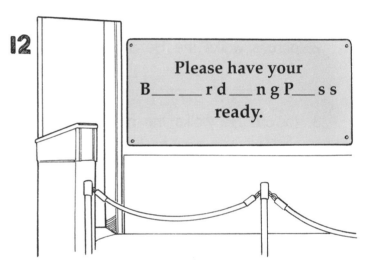

12

Please have your
B_ _ _ r d _ _ n g P_ _ s s
ready.

3.
STATE AIRLINES
T _ _ C _ _ _ T COUNTER

TICKETED PASSENGERS

4.
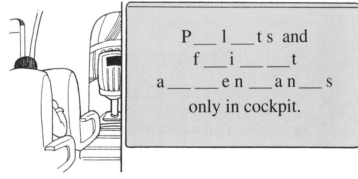

P_ _ l _ _ t s and
f_ _ i _ _ _ t
a_ _ _ _ e n _ _ a n_ _ s
only in cockpit.

5.
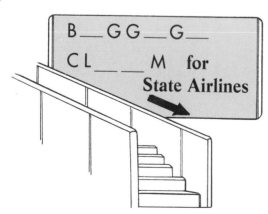
B_ _ GG_ _ G_ _
CL_ _ _ _ M for
State Airlines

6.
G_ _ _ _ _   45
Flight 2010   Chicago   12:15

CHECK-
IN

C. Read the story.

Look in your dictionary.

Underline the dictionary words in the story.

Mr. and Mrs. Fong are at the <u>airport</u> to meet their daughter, Sue, and her new husband, Ken. They wait at gate 45A.

When they see the plane arrive, Mrs. Fong waves out the window. Sue and Ken come through the gate. Mrs. Fong runs to Sue and hugs her. Mr. Fong shakes hands with Ken. Sue and Ken pick up their luggage at the baggage claim. Then they all leave the airport and go home.

D. Put the sentences from the story in the correct order.

____ a. Mr. Fong shakes hands with Ken.

__I__ b. The Fongs arrive at the airport.

____ c. Mrs. Fong hugs Sue.

____ d. The plane arrives at the airport.

____ e. Sue and Ken pick up their luggage at the baggage claim.

____ f. The Fongs wait at gate 45A.

____ g. Sue and Ken walk through the gate.

★E. Write your answers.

1. Do you like to fly? _____

2. Do you go to the airport often? _____

A. Look in your dictionary.

Write the correct word.

1. A pharmacist is also a _____ .

2. A hairdresser is also a _____ .

B. Match the occupation to the location.

1. A librarian works in a . . .   _____ a. barber shop

2. A butcher works in a . . .   _____ b. beauty salon

3. A pharmacist works in a . . .   _____ c. butcher shop

4. A mechanic works in a . . .   _____ d. dentist's office

5. A hairdresser works in a . . .   _____ e. fruit and vegetable market

6. A barber works in a . . .   __|__ f. library

7. A dental assistant works in a . . .   _____ g. drugstore

8. A grocer works in a . . .   _____ h. gas station

C. Label the picture.

3. _____

4. _____

2. _____

1. Sanitation worker

5. _____

D. **Look at the map.**

Write the missing streets.

			AVE.			AVE.			AVE.
1	2			3	4		5	6	

MAIN STREET

| 7 | 8 | 1ST | 9 | 10 | 2ND | 11 | 12 | 3RD |

•KEY•

1. PARK
2. BEAUTY SALON
3. LIBRARY
4. BARBER SHOP
5. GAS STATION

6. FRUIT & VEGETABLE MARKET
7. BUTCHER SHOP
8. DENTIST
9. SANITATION DEPT.
10. DRUG STORE

1. When you want to put gas in your car, go to the corner of

   <u>Main</u> and <u>Second</u> .

2. When you want to buy some vegetables, go to the corner of

   _____ and _____ .

3. When you want to take out a library book, go to the corner of

   _____ and _____ .

4. When you want to buy some aspirin, go to the corner of

   _____ and _____ .

★**E.** **Circle the words that are true for you.**

There's a
gas station
drug store
butcher shop
beauty salon
barber shop
library
near my home.

A. Look in your dictionary.

Alphabetize the occupations that end in **n.**

1. custodian

2. _____

3. _____

4. _____

5. _____

6. _____

B. Look at the pictures.

Write the missing letters.

1. pl u m b e r

2. g ___ r d ___ ___ e r

3. c ___ r ___ e n t ___ r

4. p ___ ___ n ___ e r

5. m ___ ___ e ___

6. h ___ ___ s ___ ___ e e ___ e r

C. Cross out (X) the word that doesn't belong in each line.

1. taxi driver   bus driver   train conductor   lock~~s~~mith

2. doorman   soldier   apartment manager   superintendent

3. foreman   housekeeper   sewing machine operator   factory worker

4. farmer   painter   construction worker   electrician

5. janitor   custodian   maintenance man   fisherman

D. Read the clues.

Unscramble the word.

1. They farm.   marfers   _farmers_

2. They keep house.   esheupeskore   _____

3. They garden.   rendaregs   _____

4. They drive taxis.   atxi vedrirs   _____

5. They drive a bus.   sub redivrs   _____

6. They paint houses.   trepinas   _____

★E. Write your answers.

1. What was your job in your country?

   I was $\begin{smallmatrix} a \\ an \end{smallmatrix}$ _____ .

2. What do you want to do in this country?

   I want to be $\begin{smallmatrix} a \\ an \end{smallmatrix}$ _____ .

A. Look in your dictionary.

Put the words in the correct box.

actor   actress   businessman   businesswoman
lawyer   messenger   reporter

Men and Women	Women	Men
lawyer		

B. Match the workers to the things they work with.

a. artist   b. babysitter   c. computer programmer

d. dancer   e. file clerk   f. photographer

g. salesperson   h. singer   i. typist

 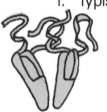 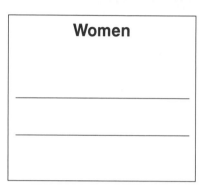 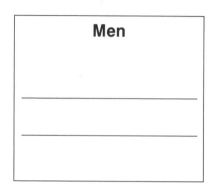

1. __i__   2. _____   3. _____   4. _____   5. _____

6. _____   7. _____   8. _____   9. _____

★C. Write your answers.

Who is your favorite singer? _____

Who is your favorite artist? _____

A. Look in your dictionary.

Write the number.

How many workers are at the construction site? _____

How many workers are putting in a window? _____

B. Read the story.

Look in your dictionary.

Underline the dictionary words in the story.

George Martin is the foreman at a <u>construction site</u>. He oversees all of the construction work. He watches the workers dig and the painters paint. He helps take out walls and put in windows. Sometimes he hammers in a few nails, or pours some cement. George always measures everything. George doesn't climb ladders to scrape paint. He is afraid to climb! George Martin is a great foreman on the ground.

C. What does George do?

Circle the pictures.

a.    b.    c.    d.

e.    f.   g.    h.

★D. Circle your answers.

Do you like to paint?	Yes, I do.	No I don't.
Do you like to climb ladders?	Yes, I do.	No I don't.
Do you like to measure things?	Yes, I do.	No I don't.

A. Look in your dictionary.

How many people are at work?

Men = _____   Women = _____

B. Circle the word that comes next.

1. Take care of . . .   meat   tickets   (grounds)   pipes

2. Cut . . .   meat   pools   grounds   groceries

3. Deliver . . .   houses   grounds   a bus   packages

4. Build . . .   tickets   furniture   clothes   meat

5. Sell . . .   newspapers children   mail   garbage

6. Collect . . .   pipes   tickets   pools   houses

7. Drive . . .   appliances furniture   a truck   tickets

8. Repair . . .   newspapers pipes   garbage   vegetables

C. Label the actions.

build
cut
deliver
drive
sell

a. __cut__

b. _____

c. _____

d. _____

e. _____

D. Look at the pictures.

Answer the questions.

1. What do mechanics do to this?

   <u>They fix it.</u>

2. What do salespeople do with these?

   <u>They sell them.</u>

3. What do letter carriers do with these?

   _____

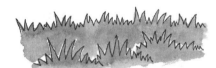

4. What do gardeners do to this?

   _____

5. What do sanitation workers do with this?

   _____

6. What do construction workers do to this?

   _____

★ **E. Write about yourself.**

1. Name something you can repair. _____

2. Name something you can sell. _____

3. Name someone you can take care of. _____

A. Look in your dictionary.

Put the words in the correct box.

| cradle crawl crib cry pacifier |
| play rattle stroller toy |

Things babies do	Places babies sleep	Things babies play with
crawl		

B. Look at the pictures and unscramble the sentences.

1. baby   playpen   the   plays   in   The

   The baby plays in the playpen.

2. goes   The   the   bottle   on   nipple

   _____

3. worker   The   dresses   the   baby   day-care

   _____

4. holds   the   The   day-care   baby   worker

   _____

5. worker   the   feeds   baby   The   day-care

   _____

C. Read the story.

Look in your dictionary.

Underline the dictionary words in the story.

I work at a day-care center. Let me tell you about a typical day. The parents drop off their children and the children cry. The crying stops and playtime begins. The babies crawl on the floor and we play with them. (I like that part of the job.) At 10:30 it's time to change diapers. (I don't like that part of the job.) At 11:00 it's lunchtime. We put bibs on the babies and give them their bottles. After lunch we change diapers again and rock the babies to sleep. At 2:00 everyone wakes up and we start all over again!

D. Read the story again.

Put the sentences in order.

_____ The workers rock the babies to sleep.

_____ The workers give the babies their bottles.

__1__ The parents drop off their babies.

_____ The babies crawl on the floor and play.

_____ The workers put bibs on the babies.

_____ The workers change the babies' diapers.

_____ The babies cry.

★E. Circle your answers.

Do you have any children?	Yes No
Can you change a diaper?	Yes No
What do you do when a baby cries?	Pick up the baby. Feed the baby. Rock the baby. Change the baby's diaper. Give the baby a pacifier. Run! Play with the baby.

A. Look in your dictionary.

How many words end in **ing** ? _____

B. Match the activity to the equipment.

a.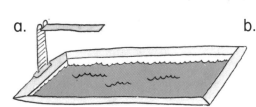

b.

c.

d.

e.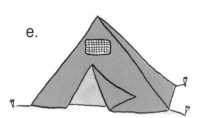

f.

g.

h.

i.

j.

k.

l.

1. _j_ play basketball   2. ___ go camping   3. ___ play tennis

4. ___ go hiking   5. ___ play an instrument   6. ___ watch TV

7. ___ go swimming   8. ___ listen to music   9. ___ play soccer

10. ___ play football   11. ___ play baseball   12. ___ go skiing

C. Write the missing words.

1.    He is going to _play tennis_ .

2.    He is going to _____ .

3.    She is going to_____ .

4.    They are going to _____ .

★D. Which activities do you do?

Make a check (✓) in the box.

	a lot	sometimes	never
I watch TV.			
I go camping.			
I go to English-speaking movies.			
I play sports.			

In my country our favorite sport is _____ .

A. Look in your dictionary.

Write two holidays that end in **day** .

_____   _____

B. Find the words and circle them.

decorate carve eat have get go make
drink paint send visit watch wear

a	p	a	b	e	d	m	a	k	e	k	e	a	t	s	v	e
s	m	o	f	d	r	i	n	k	s	l	r	v	i	s	i	t
s	p	a	i	n	t	r	e	w	a	t	c	h	k	g	e	t
g	o	m	c	a	r	v	e	e	b	c	u	s	e	n	d	e
w	e	a	r	j	h	a	v	e	d	e	c	o	r	a	t	e

C. Circle the answer.

1. Can you eat an egg?   Yes   No

2. Can you wear a parade?   Yes   No

3. Can you visit a meal?   Yes   No

4. Can you decorate a tree?   Yes   No

5. Can you carve out a pumpkin?   Yes   No

6. Can you get flowers?   Yes   No

7. Can you send a toast?   Yes   No

8. Can you get together with family? Yes   No

9. Can you drink a valentine?   Yes   No

10. Can you wave a flag?   Yes   No

Basic Oxford Picture Dictionary / Workbook

D. Write the name of the holiday.

1. In February, adults and children give valentines.

   Sometimes people get flowers. _Valentine's Day_

2. In November, many people get together with friends and family.

   They give thanks and eat a big meal. _____

3. On December 31, people celebrate with friends and family.

   They drink champagne and make a toast. _____

4. In October, children wear costumes. They carve out a pumpkin

   and go trick-or-treating. _____

5. In December, people send cards. They go shopping for presents

   or make them. _____

6. In May, people watch a special parade. They wave the flag.

   _____

7. In July, people have a barbeque or a picnic during the day.

   At night, they watch fireworks. _____

8. In March or April, children paint eggs and go on an egg hunt.

   They wear new clothes. _____

★E. Write about yourself.

I can send cards on _____ .

I can watch a parade on _____ .

I can watch fireworks on _____ .

My favorite American holiday is _____ .

Answer Key

Unit 1

2–3 An ESL Classroom

A. How many students do you see? 15

B. Write the words on the line.

a. board b. computer c. teacher d. chair e. desk
f. student g. notebook h. book

C. Write the words in the correct box.

Actions: close, listen, look, open, point to, sit, stand, talk, work.

Things: chair, computer, desk, notebook, paper, pen, pencil, window

D. Circle the correct word.

1. paper 2. book 3. chair 4. board

4 Time: Months and Seasons

A. Match the season to the month.

1. c 2. d 3. a 4. b

B. Write in the missing months.

1. May 2. April 3. July 4. June 5. October
6. August

5 Time: A Calendar

A. Write the days of the week on the calendar.

Sunday, Monday, Tuesday, Wednesday, Thursday, Friday, Saturday

6 Time: Times of Day

A. Fill in the puzzle.

Across	Down
1. afternoon	4. morning
2. evening	5. moon
3. stars	6. night
	7. sun

7 Time: The Clock

A. How many clocks do you see? 8

B. Write the correct time on the clocks below.

1. 4:00 2. 10:00 3. 2:30 4. 3:15 5. 7:00
6. 8:15 7. 12:00 8. 9:30 9. 1:15 10. 5:30
11. 12:00 12. 11:00

8 Weather

A. Alphabetize the words that end in y.

1. cloudy 2. foggy 3. icy 4. sunny 5. windy

B. Match the clothing pictures to the sentences below.

1. c 2. a 3. b 4. d

C. Complete the sentences.

1. warm 2. cool 3. hot 4. cold 5. freezing

9 Shapes and Colors

A. Alphabetize the colors that begin with b.

1. beige 2. black 3. blue 4. brown

B. Write the word in the correct box.

1. blue, gray, white black

2. triangle, square, triangle, circle

C. Write the colors.

1. red 2. white 3. yellow 4. brown 5. black 6. green

10 Money

A. Write the word under the picture.

1. penny 2. dime 3. nickel

B. Write the word.

1. dimes 2. quarter 3. a dollar, quarter

C. Unscramble the sentences.

1. The check is for $15.00. 2. The bill is for $40.00.

3. The receipt is for $1.75.

Unit 2

11. People

A. Match the word to the picture.

1. c 2. d 3. e 4. b 5. a

B. Write the words.

1. child 2. teenager 3. adult

12–13 Describing People

A. How many women do you see? 12

B. Write the words in the correct box.

Age	Hair	Height	Weight
old	blonde	short	heavy
young	wavy	tall	thin

C. Circle the correct words.

1. short, thin 2. middle aged 3. short, curly 4. tall, thin 5. young 6. long, wavy

14–15 Daily Routines

A. Alphabetize the words that begin with c.

1. comb 2. come 3. cook

B. Write the missing letters.

1. wa**sh** your f**a**ce 2. take a **sh**ower 3. **sh**ave 4. co**mb** your h**air** 5. bru**sh** your tee**th** 6. get dre**ss**ed 7. **ea**t b**r**eakf**ast**

C. Underline the dictionary words in the story.

My name is Julia Feliz. I <u>wake up</u> at 7:00 a.m. I <u>take a shower</u> and <u>get dressed</u>. I <u>eat</u> a big <u>breakfast</u> and <u>brush</u> my <u>teeth</u>. I <u>leave the house</u> at 8:00 a.m. and <u>work</u> from 8:30 a.m. to 4:30 p.m. I <u>come home</u> at 5:00 and <u>cook dinner</u>. I go to school at 6:30 and <u>study</u> English. I <u>come home</u> at 9:00 p.m. and <u>go to bed</u> at 10:30 p.m.

D. Write the times from the story.

1. 7:00 2. 8:00 3. 8:30 to 4:30 4. 5:00 5. 6:30 6. 10:30

Unit 3

16 Family

A. Put the words in the correct box.

Man	Woman	Both
father	mother	parents
grandfather	grandmother	grandparents

B. Label the picture.

(left) husband, father; son, brother

(right) wife, mother; daughter, sister

17 A Birthday Party

A. Answer the questions.

1. Yes 2. No 3. No 4. Yes 5. I don't know.

B. Fill in the puzzle.

Across	Down
1. cards	1. candles
5. Give	2. party
6. Blow	3. Sing
7. Smile	4. Open

18–19 Feelings

A. Alphabetize the words that end in y.

1. angry 2. happy 3. hungry 4. thirsty

B. Write the correct word.

1. hungry 2. tired 3. happy 4. sad 5. thirsty 6. excited

C. Underline the dictionary words in the story.

Mrs. Diego is <u>worried</u> about her family. Her husband is very <u>tired</u>. He works all the time. Her son, Miguel is <u>bored</u>. He doesn't like school. Her daughter, Flora, is <u>homesick</u>. She thinks about Mexico all the time. The children are <u>embarrassed</u> because their parents don't speak English all the time. Mr. Diego is <u>sad</u> because his children are not <u>happy</u>. Mrs. Diego is <u>scared</u> and <u>angry</u>. What is happening to her family ??!

D. Write the feelings from the story on the lines below.

Mrs. Diego	Mr. Diego	Miguel	Flora
worried	tired	bored	homesick
scared	sad	embarrassed	embarrassed
angry			

20–21 Life Events

A. Answer the questions.

1. a woman 2. a woman

B. Match the photos to the labels.

1. f 2. a 3. e 4. c 5. b 6. d

C. Answer the questions.

1. in 1956 2. in 1976 3. in 1974 4. in 1981 5. in 1993 6. in 1988

Unit 4

22 Houses and Surroundings

A. Alphabetize the words that begin with the letter g.

1. garage 2. garbage can 3. garden

B. Unscramble the sentences.

1. This is the roof.

2. This is the garbage can.

3. This is the porch.

4. This is the chimney.

5. This is the garage.

6. This is the driveway, not a backyard.

23 An Apartment Building

A. Fill in the missing letters.

1. m**a**ilbox lo**bb**y

2. int**er**c**o**m

3. el**eva**tor st**air**w**a**y fl**oo**r

4. f**ir**e esc**a**p**e**

5. h**a**ll

6. **en**tr**a**nce

24 A Living Room

A. Alphabetize the words that begin with the letter c.

1. ceiling 2. chair 3. coffee table 4. couch

B. Write the words.

a. lamp b. end table c. telephone d. stereo
e. television

25 A Kitchen

A. Write the words.

1. kitchen sink 2. cabinet 3. burner 4. oven
5. trash can 6. microwave

26 A Bedroom

A. Alphabetize the words that end in the letter t.

1. blanket 2. carpet 3. closet

B. Cross out (X) the word that doesn't belong in each line.

1. bedspread 2. alarm clock 3. pillow
4. air conditioner

27 A Bathroom

A. Write the missing words.

1. bathtub 2. sink 3. hamper 4. mirror 5. toilet
6. wastebasket 7. towel

28–29 Housework

A. Write the words in the correct box.

In the yard or garden	In the bedroom
mow the lawn	make the beds
rake the leaves	sweep the floor
water the plants	straighten up the room
plant a tree	

B. Match the picture to the word.

1. d 2. e 3. b 4. a 5. c

C. Underline the dictionary words in the story.

Everybody in the family helps <u>clean</u> the house.

On Saturday mornings they are very busy. Olga <u>makes the beds</u> and Pedro <u>cleans the bathroom.</u> The twins straighten up their bedroom.

Mrs. Vargas and her mother <u>wash and dry the</u> breakfast <u>dishes.</u> Carmen <u>dusts the furniture.</u> Mr. Vargas <u>vacuums the rugs</u> downstairs.

Outside, Grandfather <u>waters the plants.</u> His grandson Antonio <u>rakes the leaves</u> in the yard. His granddaughter Juana <u>takes out the garbage.</u>

Usually the <u>housework</u> is all done by 10:00, and then everybody can enjoy the weekend.

30 Cleaning Implements

A. Label the picture.

a. broom b. rubber gloves c. bucket d. vacuum
e. paper towels f. brush

B. Write the correct word.

1. mop

2. outlet

3. dustpan

4. cleanser

31 Tools for the Home

A. How many tools do you see? 16

B. Fill in the puzzle.

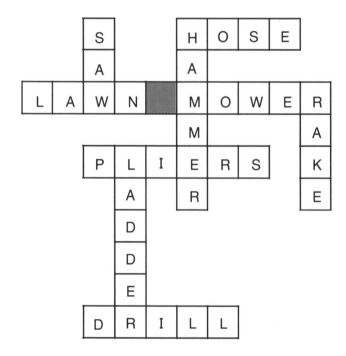

Basic Oxford Picture Dictionary / Workbook

32–33 Household Problems

A. Match the picture to the word.

a. 4 b. 3 c. 1 d. 2

B. Write the words in the correct box.

plumber

dripping faucet

stopped up toilet

flooded basement

carpenter

broken steps

broken window

leaking roof

exterminator

cockroaches

mice

C. Write the missing words.

1. window 2. toilet 3. walls 4 ceiling 5. faucet
6. sink

Unit 5

34 Vegetables

A. Alphabetize the words that begin with c.

1. cabbage 2. carrot 3. corn 4. cucumber

B. Write the missing words in this recipe.

1. onions, garlic 2. string beans, tomatoes,
mushrooms, spinach

35 Fruits

A. Alphabetize the words.

1. apples 2. bananas 3. grapes 4. oranges 5. pears

B. Write the missing letters in the ads.

1. PEACHES 2. LEMONS 3. CHERRIES
4. WATERMELON 5. STRAWBERRIES 6. PLUMS
7. GRAPEFRUIT

36 Meat and Seafood

A. How many shrimp do you see? 3

　How many clams do you see? 2

**B. Cross out (X) the word that doesn't belong in each
line.**

1. lamb 2. chicken 3. fish 4. turkey

C. Match the food to the restaurant.

1. B 2. C 3. F 4. A 5. E 6. D

37 Packaging

A. Draw a line between the words.

1. a / container / of / yogurt 2. a / package / of / cookies

3. a / carton / of / milk 4. a / bar / of / soap
5. a / bag / of / flour

B. Write the missing letters.

1. boxes 2. jar 3. loaves 4. cans 5. tubes 6. rolls

38–39 Dairy Products and Other Foods

A. Alphabetize the words that end in r.

1. butter 2. flour 3. pepper 4. sugar

B. Write the words in the correct space below.

1. butter, cheese, cream, milk, yogurt

2. cereal, ketchup, mayonnaise, mustard, rice

3. soup, milk, oil, soda, juice

4. bread, beans, flour, noodles, spaghetti

C. Circle the food words.

1. yogurt, cheese 2. bread, cookies 3. pepper, eggs,
salt 4. milk, cereal, cream 5. milk, coffee, sugar
6. margarine, bread, butter

D. Cross out the foods the man can't eat.

butter, cookies, cheese, cream, salt, sugar

40–41 Shopping at the Supermarket

A. How many people are working in the supermarket? 4

B. Write the sentence on the line.

1. A customer is pushing a cart.

2. A bagger is packing groceries.

3. The checker is weighing the apples.

4. A customer is paying for groceries.

C. Underline the dictionary words in the story.

Carol and Harry are my best underline{customers}. They come
here every Saturday morning. First they go to the
underline{bottle return}. Then they take a underline{shopping cart} and underline{push}
it down the underline{aisles}. They underline{pick out} the underline{groceries} that
they need. They underline{weigh} the fruit and vegetables on the
underline{scale}. They take their underline{groceries} to the underline{checkout
counter}. I ring up everything on the underline{cash register}.
Then Carol and Harry take the underline{bags} to their car.

Unit 6

42 A Table Setting

A. Label the picture.

a. saucer b. glass c. napkin d. fork e. plate f. cup
g. spoon h. knife

B. Write the missing words.

1. napkin 2. spoon 3. cup

43 At a Restaurant

A. Circle the answers.

1. Yes 2. Yes 3. No 4. Yes 5. No 6. No

B. Write the word in the correct box.

People who work in a restaurant	Things in a restaurant
busboy	water
cashier	booth
cook	menu
waitress	chair

44–45 Common Prepared Foods

A. Write the desserts you see.

ice cream, apple pie

B. Circle the correct words.

1. fried eggs, toast 2. hamburger, french fries
3. hot dog, ice cream 4. spaghetti, salad

C. Write the missing letters on the menu.

fruit salad	waffles
fried eggs	pancakes
scrambled eggs	syrup
sausage	sausage
	bacon

46–47 Cooking a Meal

A. Write 3 ways to cook food.

fry, bake, boil, broil, steam

B. Match the steps in the recipe to the pictures

1. e 2. c 3. b 4. a 5. d

C. Write the missing words.

1. boil 2. steam 3. fry 4. pour 5. grate 6. stir
7. bake

Unit 7

48 Basic Clothes

A. Circle the answer.

1. Yes 2. Yes 3. No 4. Yes 5. No

49 Casual Clothes

A. How many swimsuits do you see? 7

B. Alphabetize the names of these casual clothes.

1. sandals 2. shorts 3. sneakers 4. swimsuit

C. Write the missing letters.

1. swimsuit 2. sunglasses 3. sandals 4. sneakers
5. T shirt 6. baseball cap

50 Cold Weather Clothes

A. Alphabetize the words that end in the letter t.

1. coat 2. hat 3. jacket 4. raincoat 5. sweatshirt
6. vest

B. Match the word to the picture.

1. b 2. c 3. d 4. a 5. c

51 Underwear and Sleepwear

A. Alphabetize the words that begin with p.

1. pajamas 2. panties 3. pantyhose

B. Match the picture to the sentence.

1. f 2. a 3. d 4. g 5. e 6. c 7. h 8. b

52–53 Describing Clothes

A. Circle the correct words.

1. She / high / short / light

2. She / low / long / heavy

3. He / short / tight / dirty / old

4. He / wet / extra-large / wide

B. Fill in the puzzle.

1. old 2. dirty 3. narrow 4. heavy 5. high 6. wet
7. tight

54 At the Store (Prepositions I)

A. Write the correct words under the pictures.

1. sneakers 2. boots 3. sandals 4. slippers

B. Write the words.

1. between 2. in front of 3. under 4. behind

C. Follow the directions.

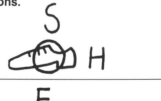

55 Jewelry and Accessories

B. Label the ad.

1. ring 2. bracelet 3. necklace 4. earrings 5. watch

56 Taking Care of Clothes: The Laundromat

A. How many washing machines do you see?   7

   How many dryers do you see?   2

B. Write the order.

1st   Load the machine.

2nd   Put detergent in the machine.

3rd   Unload the machine.

4th   Put clothes in the dryer.

5th   Fold the clothes.

57 Taking Care of Clothes: The Tailor / Dry Cleaner

A. Write the words.

1. scissors 2. zipper 3. needle 4. button
5. thread 6. hanger

Unit 8

58–59 The Body

A. Look in your Dictionary.

1. purple 2. thin

B. Write the words in the correct box.

I have one...	I have two...	I have ten...
head	legs	fingers
back	arms	toes
chest	feet	
neck	hips	

C. Cross out (X) the word that doesn't belong in each line.

1. chest 2. ankle 3. knee 4. hip 5. wrist

D. Write the missing words.

1. heart 2. brain 3. stomach 4. lungs

60 The Face and Head

A. Look in your dictionary and label the picture.

a. forehead b. eyebrow c. mouth d. chin e. hair
f. eye g. ear h. nose

B. Underline the dictionary words.

Dear Aunt Jane,

Here's a picture of our Tanya. Isn't she beautiful. She has her father's <u>eyes</u> and <u>mouth</u>. She has my <u>nose,</u> not too big, not too small. Maybe she will have the family <u>ears</u>. They are quite big. Can you see her <u>tooth</u>? It's her first <u>tooth</u>. I love it. Her <u>chin</u> is really cute too.

61 Toiletries

A. Alphabetize the words with sh.

1. brush 2. shampoo 3. shaving cream 4. toothbrush
5. washcloth

B. Write the words under the correct pictures.

comb	razor	toothbrush
brush	blades	toothpaste
shampoo		

62–63 Aches, Pains, and Injuries

A. Alphabetize the words that end in _____ache.

1. backache 2. earache 3. headache
4. stomachache 5. toothache

B. Underline the dictionary words in the story.

Thot Sok is absent from class today. He has a <u>cold</u> and a <u>sore throat</u>. He is <u>coughing</u> and <u>sneezing</u>. He has a <u>headache</u> and a <u>fever</u>. He is in bed. His daughter Tu is home too. She has an <u>insect bite</u> on her foot. Her ankle is <u>swollen</u> and her foot is <u>infected</u>. She cannot walk, so she is in bed too. Thot's wife is at the doctor's today. She has <u>high blood pressure</u> and sometimes she <u>faints</u>. Who's taking care of the baby? He has a <u>stomachache</u>.

C. Mark the picture.

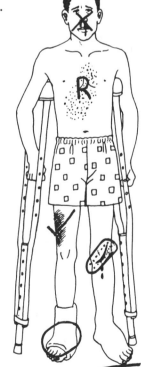

64 Treatments

A. How many kinds of medicine do you see? 5

B. Match the problems to the treatment.

1. b 2. a 3. e 4. d 5. c

65 First Aid and Health Care Items

A. Fill in the correct word.

1. crutches 2. heating pad 3. thermometer 4. Band-Aid 5. icepack 6. hot water bottle 7. wheelchair

66–67 At a Medical Office

A. Circle the answer.

1. doctor 2. nurse 3. nurse 4. doctor

B. Match the picture to the word.

1. b 2. e 3. d 4. c 5. f 6. a

C. Write what the receptionist asks a patient to do.

1. show, card 2. print, name 3. fill out, form
4. sign, name 5. wait, waiting

Unit 9

68–69 The Community

A. Fill in the missing letters.

1. police 2. bus station 3. fire station 4. train station

B. Write the missing letters.

1. city hall 2. court house 3. police station
4. bakery 5. bookstore 6. florist 7. school
8. park 9. church 10. post office

C. Underline the dictionary words in the story.

On Saturday mornings the King family drives downtown. They park the car in the <u>parking garage</u> across from the <u>post office</u>. The Kings walk to the <u>park</u> and eat their lunch. After lunch, they drive to the <u>mall</u>. First they go shopping at Stockton's <u>department store</u>. Then they go to the <u>movie theater</u>. After the movie, they stop at the <u>bakery</u> and buy some doughnuts. It's late in the afternoon when the tired but happy King family drives back home.

D. Number the pictures.

a. 4 b. 2 c. 5 d. 1 e. 6 f. 3

70 Banking

A. Write the words in the correct space below.

Places you wait at the bank	Jobs at the Bank	Things you write on a check
ATM/cash machine	security guard	amount
line	teller	date
drive-thru window		signature

B. Circle the answers.

1. $55.00 2. 7/2/04 3. 7/21/04 4. $15.00

71 The Post Office

A. Alphabetize the words that end in e.

envelope, package, zip code

B. Match the sentence to the word.

1. d 2. c 3. a 4. b

72–73 An Intersection

A. Write the number.

1. 3 2. 1

B. Match the location to the action.

1. c 2. a 3. d 4. f 5. e 6. b

C. Label the picture.

1. bench 2. bus stop 3. parking meter 4. crosswalk
5. pedestrian 6. newsstand 7. curb

D. Circle the correct picture.

1. b 2. a 3. a 4. a 5. a 6. a

74–75 Emergencies and Natural Disasters

A. Write the words in the correct box.

Emergencies	Occupations
accident	fire fighter
fire	paramedic
robbery	police officer
mugging	

B. Label the natural disasters.

1. tornado 2. flood 3. hurricane 4. earthquake

D. Write the correct word.

1. choke 2. fall. 3. drown. 4. heart attack.
5. swallow poison. 6. fire.

Unit 10

76 Transportation

A. Answer the questions.

white and orange, orange

B. Write the word.

1. car 2. motorcycle 3. bus 4. bicycle 5. plane
6. taxi cab

77 Parts of a Car

A. Write the words in the correct box.

On the car	Inside the car
license plate	accelerator
tire	dashboard
windshield	steering wheel

B. Fill in the puzzle.

Across
1. battery
2. headlights
5. trunk
6. seat

Down
1. brake
2. hood
3. ignition
4. seatbelt
7. gas tank

78–79 On the Road (Prepositions II)

A. Write the answers.

1. purple 2. brown 3. green

B. Match the picture to the description.

1. c 2. e 3. a 4. f 5. b 6. d

C. Unscramble the sentences.

1. He walks away from the school.
2. He walks across the street.
3. He walks toward the market.
4. He goes into the market.
5. He walks out of the market.
6. He goes around the corner.
7. He walks up the steps and into the house.

80–81 At an Airport

A. Alphabetize the words that end in e.

1. arrive 2. baggage 3. gate 4. leave 5. luggage
6. shake 7. suitcase 8. wave

B. Write the missing letters in each sign.

1. passengers 2.Boarding Pass 3.Ticket 4. Pilots/
flight attendants 5. Baggage Claim 6. Gate

C. Underline the dictionary words in the story.

Mr. and Mrs. Fong are at the airport to meet their
daughter, Sue and her new husband, Ken. They wait
at gate 45A. When they see the plane arrive, Mrs.
Fong waves out the window. Sue and Ken come
through the gate. Mrs. Fong runs to Sue and hugs her.
Mr. Fong shakes hands with Ken. Sue and Ken pick up
their luggage at the baggage claim. Then they all leave
the airport and go home.

D. Put the sentences from the story in the correct order.

a. 6 b. 1 c. 5 d. 3 e. 7 f. 2 g. 4

Unit 11

82–83 Occupations and Workplaces I

A. Write the correct word.

1. druggist 2. hair stylist

B. Match the occupation to the location.

1. f 2. c 3. g 4. h 5. b 6. a 7. d 8. e

C. Label the picture.

1. sanitation worker 2. doorman 3. dentist 4. grocer
5. delivery person.

D. Answer the questions.

1. Main, Second 2. Main, Third 3. Main, First
4. Main, Second

84–85 Occupations II

A. Alphabetize the occupations that end in n.

1. custodian 2. doorman 3. electrician 4. fisherman
5. foreman 6. maintenance man

B. Write the missing letters.

1. plumber 2. gardener 3. carpenter 4. painter
5. mover 6. housekeeper

**C. Cross out (X) the word that doesn't belong in each
line.**

1. locksmith 2. soldier 3.housekeeper 4. farmer
5. fisherman

D. Read the clues and unscramble the word.

1. farmers 2. housekeepers 3. gardeners
4. taxi drivers 5. bus drivers 6. painters

86 Occupations III

A. Put the words in the correct box.

Men and Women	Women	Men
lawyer	actress	actor
messenger	businesswoman	businessman
reporter		

B. Match the workers to the things they work with.

1. i 2. c 3. d 4. h 5. a 6. f 7. e 8. b 9. g

87 A Construction Site

A. Answer the questions.

How many workers are at the construction site?   13

How many workers are putting in a window?   2

B. Underline the dictionary words in the story.

George Martin is the foreman at a <u>construction site</u>. He <u>oversees</u> all of the construction work. He watches the workers <u>dig</u> and the painters <u>paint</u>. He helps <u>take out</u> walls and <u>put in</u> windows. Sometimes he <u>hammers</u> in a few nails, or <u>pours</u> some cement. George always <u>measures</u> everything. George doesn't <u>climb</u> ladders to <u>scrape</u> paint. He is afraid to climb! George Martin is a great foreman on the ground.

C. Circle the pictures.

b, d, f, h

88–89 At Work

A. Count the men and women.

Men = 16, Women = 7

B. Circle the word that comes next.

1. grounds 2. meat 3. packages 4. furniture
5. newspapers 6. tickets 7. a truck 8. pipes

C. Label the actions.

1. cut 2. sell 3. build 4. drive 5. deliver

D. Answer the questions.

1. They fix it. 2. They sell them. 3. They deliver them.
4. They cut it. 5. They collect it. 6. They build it.

90–91 A Day-Care Center

A. Put these words in the correct box.

Things babies do	Places babies sleep	Things babies play with
crawl	cradle	pacifier
cry	crib	rattle
play	stroller	toy

B. Look at the pictures and unscramble the sentences.

1. The baby plays in the playpen.
2. The nipple goes on the bottle.
3. The day-care worker dresses the baby.
4. The day-care worker holds the baby.
5. The day-care worker feeds the baby.

C. Underline the dictionary words in the story.

I work at a <u>day-care</u> center. Let me tell you about a typical day. The parents <u>drop off</u> their children and the children <u>cry</u>. The crying stops and playtime begins. The babies <u>crawl</u> on the floor and we <u>play</u> with them. (I

like that part of the job). At 10:30 it's time to <u>change diapers</u>. (I don't like that part of the job.) At 11:00 it's lunchtime. We put <u>bibs</u> on the babies and give them their <u>bottles</u>. After lunch we <u>change diapers</u> again and <u>rock</u> the babies to sleep. At 2:00 everyone wakes up and we start all over again!

D. Put the sentences in order.

1. The parents drop off their babies.
2. The babies cry.
3. The babies crawl on the floor and play.
4. The workers change the babies' diapers.
5. The workers put bibs on the babies.
6. The workers give the babies their bottles.
7. The workers rock the babies to sleep.

Unit 12

92–93 Leisure

A. How many words end in ing? 5

B. Match the activity to the equipment.

1. j 2. e 3. l 4. f 5. c 6. b 7. a 8. g 9. h 10. i 11. k 12. d

C. Write the words.

1. play tennis 2. play baseball 3. play basketball
4. go to the movies

94–95 Celebrate the Holidays

A. Write two holidays that end in day.

Valentine's Day, Memorial Day

B. Find the words and circle them.

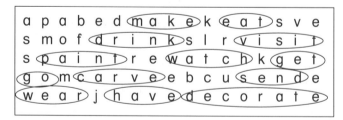

C. Circle the answer.

1. Yes 2. No 3. No 4. Yes 5. Yes 6. Yes 7. No
8. Yes 9. No 10. Yes

D. Write the holiday.

1. Valentine's Day 2. Thanksgiving 3. New Year's Day 4. Halloween 5. Christmas 6. Memorial Day
7. Fourth of July 8. Easter